X60

X60

ROTHMANS
WIMBLEDON ON CAMERA

Arthur Cole's pictorial history of the world's greatest tennis tournament

Researched and Designed by **Robert Duncan**

Story by **Lance Tingay**

Foreword by **Dan Maskell**

Arthur Cole's biography by **Jack Prosser**

Edited by **Geoff Peters**

Rothmans Publications Limited

Published in Great Britain
by Rothmans Publications Limited,
Oxford Road, Aylesbury, Bucks.

ISBN 0 907574 04 1

Phototypesetting by Getset (BTS) Ltd, Eynsham, Oxford.
Set in 10/11 pt. Lubalin Extra Light.
Printed in Great Britain by K L Litho Ltd.

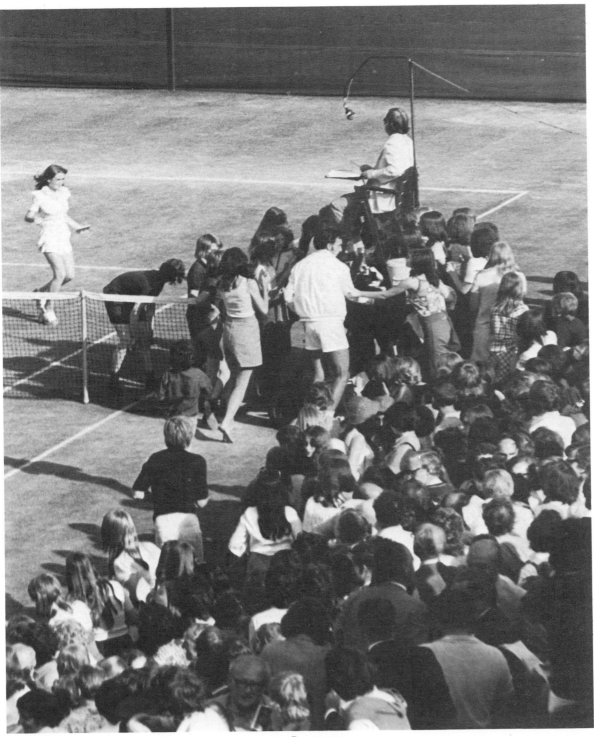

Foreword

I have known Arthur Cole
for well over 40 years. He
used to take pictures of me
when we had Davis Cup
training sessions in the pre-
war days. Even then, he
was one of the few
specialist tennis photographers — probably because
he was a good player
himself and developed a
sense of action awareness
so important in a game
like tennis.

He has so many friends
throughout the world of
tennis that it is difficult to
find someone connected
with the game who doesn't
know him. I think that it is
fair to say he is one of the
world's best photographers
of action tennis.

His work with his camera
has taken him to all the
world's major tennis events,
and to some that have
proved to be not quite so
major. His standards,
though, are unfailingly
high and we in tennis
know him as a true pro-
fessional. We also know
him as a man whose sense
of fun is as welcome as his
ability to take fine pictures.

While he has covered all
the famous tennis tourna-
ments, it is his unique
association with the
greatest event there is,
Wimbledon, that is quite
rightly the subject of this
book. I am sure that everyone wishes him great
success with it and we all
look forward to seeing him
at many more tourna-
ments in the future,
especially at Wimbledon.

Dan Maskell.

13

About Arthur Cole

If you are lucky enough to get tickets for the Centre Court at Wimbledon on Finals Day, spare a moment or two to look at the Press photographers. You will notice a slight, sun-tanned figure who tends to stand out because he looks, well, smart, I suppose is the only word. That is Arthur Cole. Rarely without a jacket, never without a tie, he believes that Finals Day is an occasion and that one should dress for it.

Watch too, as the photographers rush and jostle to take the pictures of the presentation. Somehow or another, Arthur Cole always seems to achieve a prime position. How does he do it? 'I don't know,' he says, 'it just seems to happen.'

It is that ability to be in the right place at the right time that has secured his place as one of the world's leading tennis photographers.

Born in 1920 in Wallasey, Cheshire, he attended Wallasey Grammar School. In the early 1930's, the family moved south to Beckenham in Kent. Apart from his war services, he has never left the area, but there is still that trace of the Wirral burr in his voice.

Arthur Cole did not follow in his father's

14

footsteps. Instead of opting for music as his career, he studied industrial design. He served an 'apprenticeship' with the Industrial Design Partnership in Bedford Square, London as well as studying at art school. All this resulted in qualifying him for the Royal College of Arts examination in industrial design.

While studying was going on, the young Cole was also busy in another field . . . tennis. In the modern idiom, Arthur Cole was a tennis buff. A member of Shirley Park Tennis Club, he was a frequent — and successful — participant in Junior Tournaments.

He played at Wimbledon; not in the tournaments, to be sure, but he played there. It was, clearly, his own native ability at the game that gave him such an insight into the very specialised business of taking action pictures of tennis.

Around the age of 14, another very important event took place — Arthur Cole bought a camera. It was a Zeiss-Ikon, 'with bellows,' he hastens to explain. The object was to take snaps but he ended up taking tennis pictures and very rapidly was into the business of developing and printing his own pictures.

He was meticulous with those pictures. They were carefully documented and filed away. In 1935, the editor of a magazine called 'Lawn Tennis and Badminton' happened to see some of them and bought them on the spot, including some taken in 1934. It was the start of a long and distinguished career that was to make Arthur Cole the best-known name in tennis photography.

with Fred Perry

While tennis and, of course, photography played a very important part in his life in those pre-war days, there were other things to do. Like earning a living as an industrial designer, which he proceeded to do, in part while he was still qualifying.

In 1939, yet another interest was taken up. Arthur Cole joined the Royal Air Force Volunteer Reserve. Those were the days, of course, when in the time-hallowed phrase 'the storm clouds were gathering over Europe'. But, as he explains, he did not join the RAFVR out of a deep and burning sense of patriotism, although one senses that this now unfashionable emotion did play an important part in the exercise. 'No,' says Cole, 'I joined because I wanted to learn to fly.' Well, he did learn to fly and, at the same time as coping with tennis, industrial design and his newish status as a paid photographer, he also found time to join with Jimmy Jones and Murray Delaford (both Davis Cup players) to become a director of 'British Lawn Tennis', a monthly magazine devoted to the game that has played such a dominant role in his life. Both Jimmy Jones and his parents played an important part in helping Arthur Cole in his tennis career.

And there were cars. Anyone who has been driven by Arthur Cole can testify to the fact that he drives rather fast. 'I always wanted to be a racing driver,' he confesses, 'but then I had a go and decided it was not for me.' Still, in those halcyon days before 1939, there were plenty of cars around to take a young man's fancy. His fancy was taken with M.G.s — five of them. In fact, something like 70-odd cars have taken his fancy over the years, ranging from a Bentley, through Rolls-Royce, to a brace of Ferrari sports cars.

The onset of war put a stop to Wimbledon and to his industrial design work, for the young pilot was rather rapidly required by the R.A.F. As a pilot he flew all types of aircraft and in 1943 he was sent to the Air Ministry where he found his photographic skills further developed in the field of aerial photography. He was also 'on loan' to the Ministry of Aircraft production and was an assistant to Peter Masefield, the man who was later to head Britain's national airline.

Arthur Cole reckons that his time with the Ministries was invaluable to his development as a photographer. At the start of the war aerial photography was fairly basic. By the end of the war it had become a highly developed and highly specialised business that was to play a vital role in so many aspects of the conflict.

Although tennis had to take a back-seat generally, there were still at least some opportunities to play. He took part in a couple of Red Cross Exhibition Matches, but a back injury received in crash-landing put paid to any hopes of playing serious tennis for Arthur Cole.

During the war, he also met and married an attractive WAAF from 11 Group Intelligence. That was in 1944 and Hazel Cole now has her own involvement in tennis.

In the post-war period he was back in the industrial design business working with Godfrey Imhof on a variety of projects, including radios. But always, there was the tennis photography. . . . 'I was always taking pictures,' he says. Of course, the ability to take pictures helped enormously with the design work.

In common with other photographers, he used a plate camera in his pre-war days. However, he quickly saw the advantage of lighter equipment and in 1938 he bought a 35mm Leica. According to Cole, he reckons he was 'the first one to use a 35mm camera at Wimbledon' and that Leica saw sterling service as soon as the Wimbledon tournaments started again. For the past 20 years, he has used Nikon equipment, a decision arrived at after trying out many other cameras. The reason? 'They are the best,' says Cole.

Eventually, it dawned on Arthur Cole that the picture business demanded a somewhat more formal approach and that there was considerable potential in industrial design as well. So he left Godfrey Imhof and formed two companies of his own — one for industrial design and the other for photography called Le-Roye which is still going strong. As part of his industrial design activities, he was involved in a wide range of products, including the first power boat, in conjunction with Ray Hunt, for the Cowes–Torquay race for Tommy Sopwith and Bruce Campbell. Apart from his photographic business and his industrial design, he started a tennis magazine back in the early 1960's. Called 'Tennis World', it was destined to become one of the more influential magazines in the game around the world. Fortunately for Arthur Cole, his daughter Suzie helped him with the magazine. Of course, as part of the Cole family she already knew many of the world's tennis stars. On 'Tennis World' she became no mean tennis journalist, interviewing all the great international players, and played a vital role in running the magazine.

So by the mid-60's, Cole was running a successful photographic business and an expanding magazine as well as operating as an industrial designer. He says of that time, 'I never seemed to find the time to sleep, except on planes.'

Ten years on, and with increasing pressures of business, he happened to be in New York talking to superstar agent Mark McCormack about 'Tennis World'; they agreed terms and it was eventually sold. Arthur Cole had cut his commitments by one third.

Now he is handing over the Le-Roye business to his son Michael. He did follow in his father's footsteps and is a highly-regarded tennis photographer in his own right as well as being a vital part of the business.

Some people might feel that the time has now come to take things a little easier. Not Arthur Cole. He is involved in yet another project concerning the game he loves. He is a consultant to the Grand Prix International Racquet Club, the £2 million racquets sports centre in Coventry, as well as being a director.

As he says, 'I shall take pictures at Wimbledon as long as I can hold a camera'. Well, 45 years is some record. Perhaps we can look forward to not only a golden issue of 'Wimbledon on Camera', but a diamond issue as well.

Jack Prosser

Suzie Cole (with Colin Dibley)

Arthur Cole (with Mrs Hewitt and Mrs Newcombe)

Barker

Austin

17

Mandlikova

Jaeger

Evert

19

King

Wade

Navratilova

Budge

Borotra

Emerson

Ashe

Hoad (with Peter Ustinov)

Smith

Ramirez

Tanner

Nastase

27

Gerulaitis

Pecci

29

Borg

31

THE WIMBLEDON STORY
by
LANCE TINGAY

THE LAST BRITISH GLORIES
1934-1945

At the time, 1934 looked like the start of a new era — the revival of Wimbledon to old patriotic glories. The Lawn Tennis Championships were being staged for the 54th time in all. It was for the 13th time at "New Wimbledon", that is, the present site in Church Road to which it had moved from Worple Road in 1922. There were still people nostalgically claiming that the strawberries and cream at the old venue were better.

New Wimbledon or not, there had been no British men's singles winner since Arthur Gore (at the age of 41!) in 1909.

"Britain's Year At Last" went the headlines. A very pushing player, Fred Perry, who had been born in the year Gore had last won, triumphed. The next day a rather prim young lady, Dorothy Round, a Sunday School teacher from the Midlands, won the women's singles.

These stirring happenings climaxed a meeting that had been blessed with baking heat and fraught with the infection of a virus called "Wimbledon throat". Players were affected by the score, spectators in hundreds, and a nasty, if brief, fever it was. One of the favourites, the German Baron Gottfried Von Cramm, was beaten because of it. Jack Crawford, the defending men's champion — and a superb classic stylist — survived a bout before falling to Perry in the final.

Times were changing. Only five years earlier the South African Billie Tapscott had appeared on the Centre Court without stockings — and before Queen Mary, too! Only the year before, Bunny Austin, the British number two, had had the boldness to play on the same sacred location in shorts!

The sartorial innovation could not have been brought about by a more respectable person. Austin was ex-Repton and Cambridge.

Perry, quite apart from his dash and flair, will to win and zeal for fitness, was different. He had been to a grammar school. And in writing of him in his early days one had to make the point that he was the son of an M.P. — a Labour M.P.!

From 1934 to 1936, Perry dominated Wimbledon. There were chauvinistic glories all round. In the last year, Perry not only took his third singles title, but his Davis Cup colleagues, Pat Hughes and Raymond Tuckey, won the men's doubles. The British pair, Freda James and Kay Stammers, won the women's doubles, this for the second year. Perry also partnered Miss Round to

Perry.

take the mixed doubles for the second time.

That was four championships out of five for Great Britain.

1935 was memorable for the manner of Helen's seventh championship. There was only one Helen, Helen Wills Moody from Berkeley, California, and invincible year after year. "Poker Face Helen" she was called, for not a trace of emotion, whether joy or misery, did she ever reveal. Such a cold fish was not loved, but she was admired.

Her rival — and bitter rival of a lifetime — was Helen II. She was Helen Jacobs, also from Berkeley, California. Her ambition was to beat Helen I.

She had lost on countless occasions. But if Helen II were to win, what could be sweeter than on the occasion that matters most? In the final of 1935 Miss Jacobs met her arch foe. Mrs. Moody had, in an early round, actually dropped a set to an 18 year-old Czech, Slecna Cepkova. Her invincibility had shed its thickest armour. Miss Jacobs, as inspired as Mrs. Moody was jaded, led 5-2 in the third set. At 5-3 she reached match point and needed only to kill a short lob into a vacant court to fulfill the toil of years. A slight gust of wind combined with nerves to make Miss Jacobs fluff the shot.

Mrs. Moody accordingly won her singles title number seven. In 1936 Miss Jacobs won in her rival's absence and it was almost an empty glory. The year following, 1937, the gallant Miss Round triumphed for the second time. But by then British glories were fading. Perry turned professional.

The only player who really mattered in 1937 and 1938 was the red-headed Don Budge. He was from California. His father was from Scotland and had played for Glasgow Rangers, giving him a distinguished sporting lineage. Budge was a powerhouse of tennis skill and his backhand, where he took the ball almost as early as Perry did on the forehand, was projected with a rolled top spin that was devastating.

Budge made himself the first triple champion in 1937. He improved on the feat the following year with a standard of performance that was awesome. The singles he won without the loss of a set and he yielded only one set in all three events, that in the final of the men's doubles.

He helped set another record. All five championships were taken by Americans. Mrs. Moody won the women's singles for the eighth time, another unique achievement.

As Budge strode so commandingly about the Wimbledon courts he did so as the first Grand Slam winner in history. That achievement, holding the four major championships at the same time, was brought about as soon as he had taken the French title in June.

Budge turned professional in 1938. Nevertheless, 1939 was a year equally dominated by Americans. Alice Marble was the women's champion. Though plagued by ill health, this none-the-less athletic Californian took women's technique to new dimensions. Her serve and volley were almost masculine. She became triple champion.

So did Bobby Riggs, a fine touch player. 1939 was his first and only Wimbledon. He coolly backed himself to win all three events and never looked like losing his bet. If he lacked the greatness of Budge he owed nothing to anyone in confidence.

Budge, in turning professional, did so for a guarantee of $50,000. To players just before World War II it was a lot of money.

The seeds of a modern Wimbledon had been firmly planted. The first radio commentaries had been broadcast in 1927. A decade later, 1937, television transmissions were made.

Fred Perry arguably the greatest British player of all time, had the first of his dominating Wimbledon victories in 1934.

1934

In 1934 the bowler hat and umbrella still betokened the smart Englishman who looked in at Wimbledon having spent the morning in his office.

1934

Fred Perry, fit, lissome and
dedicated to winning, won
The Championship at his
sixth attempt in 1934 and
subsequently never lost a
singles.

1934

Fred Perry had his second
year of singles invincibility

1935

The Queen to be and the
Queen who was in 1935.
The Duchess of York, later
Queen Elizabeth, and
Helen Wills Moody who
won the singles for seventh
time and was 'Queen
Helen'.

1935

Professional Dan Maskell
became the leading British
coach when appointed to
the All England Club in
1928. Here he is with Kay
Stammers

1936

Sarah Palfrey and her
doubles partner Helen Jacobs

1936

The British idol Kay
Stammers (on the left)
clashed with the American
Helen Jacobs (right) in the
women's doubles final 1936.
Kay and Freda James beat
Helen and Sarah Fabyan
6–2 6–1.

1936

Regular Army officer
Raymond Tuckey became
one of Britain's best doubles
players in the 1930's.

1936

Fred Perry won the singles
for the third successive
year in 1936, overwhelming
the German Baron
Gottfried Von Cramm 6–1
6–1 6–0.

1936

Don Budge, the champion
of 1937. He also won in 1938
and took 'The Grand Slam'.

1937

47

Helen Wills Moody (left)
won the singles for a
record eighth time in 1938.
In the quarter-final she
beat Britain's Kay
Stammers (right) 6–2 6–1.

1938

Dorothy Little (the
champion as Miss Round
in 1934 and 1937) and her
fourth round conqueror
Sarah Palfrey Fabyan

1939

Sarah Palfrey Fabyan won
the women's doubles for
the second year with Alice
Marble

1939

Kay Stammers, a much
loved British favourite,
raised hopes by reaching
the singles final in 1939. She
was overwhelmed 6–2
6–0 by Alice Marble.

1939

Alice Marble, after fighting
ill health for years, won all
three events at a
triumphant Wimbledon

1939

THE AMERICAN DECADE
1946-1955

Wimbledon in 1946 picked up where it left off in 1939 — more or less. Some 1,200 seats round the Centre Court had been lost, for the All England Club had not escaped the Blitz and the hole left by a 500lb bomb was not repaired until the following year.

The crowds were denser than ever. The clothes rationing in force had little effect on the colourful parade of outré fashion. In 1948 the crowd on the first Saturday exceeded 33,000 and so frightening was the density it provoked subsequent limitation.

The game's middle-class image persisted in some degree but could not resist the social changes of Britain. The happenings of 1949 were significant.

Moran

In that year, dress designer Ted Tinling produced lace panties for the American Gussie Moran — "Gorgeous Gussie". It marked the transition from an old world to a new. Even so, the wide publicity did not meet with universal approval. In particular Sir Louis Greig, the chairman of the Wimbledon Management Committee, did not renew Tinling's job as the players' liaison officer responsible for getting the competitors on the show courts, a post he had held for years.

The men's singles champion in 1946 was the tall Frenchman, Yvon Petra, his win reflecting the unsettled form in the aftermath of the war. The United States, however, was the one country where interruption to lawn tennis had been minimal. For a decade it was rare for any but an American player to make a really effective show at Wimbledon.

The astonishing statistic of the post-war decade is that, out of the 50 championship titles that were decided, no less than 38 were either won or shared by Americans. Among women, 40 places in the semi-finals of the singles were filled. Only one was not American.

Jack Kramer, the best of the Americans, would probably have won in 1946 had he not developed a blistered hand and lost to Jaroslav Drobny, a Czech who had dis-

Drobny

tinguished himself as a 16 year-old before the war by taking Budge to five sets in Prague. Kramer came into his own in 1947 with vengeance.

The final was remarkable in that he devastated his compatriot Tom Brown 6-1 6-3 6-2 in a mere 48 minutes. He did not match Budge's pre-war record by taking the singles without the loss of a set, for he lost one; but in winning 130 games and losing only 37 he set a record of superiority that is unique.

Kramer turned professional and Bob Falkenburg, who succeeded him as champion in 1948, was hardly popular. For one, there was his habit of conserving his lanky energies by blatantly "throwing" sets. For another, his final opponent, John Bromwich, was the best-loved Australian of all time.

He was ambidexterous and double-fisted and had an angelic touch with an absurdly light racket lightly strung. This gentle giant led 5-2, 40-15 in the fifth set. He turned to the ball boy and said, "Give me the winning ball". Falkenburg produced the all-or-nothing passing shots of a gambler to save three match balls and won the title.

There was as precarious an American winner in 1949 when the ambling, pipe-smoking Ted Schroeder paid his only Wimbledon visit. On a broiling middle Saturday he met Frank Sedgman, then an up and coming Australian, on Court One and was twice match point down. On the first, Schroeder was footfaulted and he then came up to make a winning volley from his second service. While two years before Kramer was the easiest champion, Schroeder was the most laboured. He dropped eight sets in all and his eventual margin was 172 games to 119.

Gonzales

It was that year that Richard Gonzales won his only Wimbledon title, taking the men's doubles with Frank Parker. Most felt he could have been a singles champion had he come back but he turned pro-fessional.

The sequence of American women's singles champions was led in the first post-war year by Pauline Betz, a great player in every aspect. Early the following year she had talks, no more, about turning pro-fessional. The U.S. Association promptly declared she had forfeited her amateur status and, willy-nilly, she was a professional anyway! Margaret Osborne, who later became Mrs. du Pont, followed her. Then came her doubles partner Louise Brough. What a player and what a career!

In 1948 she was triple champion and in 1949 she was again a triple finalist. She lost just the mixed. There was never anything like her last Saturday effort. In the singles she beat Mrs. du Pont 10-8 1-6 10-8 (at that time the second longest final played). In the doubles she and Mrs. du Pont beat Gussie Moran and Pat Todd 8-6 7-5. In the mixed, the South Africans Eric Sturgess and Sheila Summers beat Bromwich and Miss Brough 9-7 9-11 7-5.

Louise Brown played eight sets and 117 games that finals day! And she never turned a hair!

A year later she was again triple champion, having won eight out of nine finals in three years. Like Alice Marble she never hit a ground stroke if she could play a volley.

American talent spilled over itself during these years. In 1951 there was again a triple champion from the United States, the much-loved Doris Hart, majestic in her stroking and as graceful a player as ever trod the court. Yet her legs were partially deformed and as a child she had taken up the game as a remedial exercise.

Patty

To become men's singles champion Budge Patty, a GI who had never gone back from Europe to America, trained to the extent of giving up smoking and doubled the French title with that at Wimbledon in 1950. No-one ever played a forehand volley better. Richard Savitt, who succeeded him, conquered at his first attempt.

In 1952 the line of American success in the men's singles was broken. The Australian Frank Sedgman had his triumph and did rather more. He won all three championship titles, the only man in Wimbledon's post-war history to do so.

In the same year history began to be written by Maureen Connolly. She came as a 17 year-old who had won her own title the previous autumn when only 16. The imprint of invincibility was all over her. Her volleying was nothing. Her ground strokes, and markedly her backhand, were shatteringly good.

She came to Wimbledon under the wing of her coach, "Teach Tennant", a woman of strong and, as it turned out, over-protective personality. When Miss Connolly hurt her shoulder she wanted her to scratch. The 17 year-old immediately made her own decision to go on, threw away her tutelage and called the press together to announce it.

Two rivals, the British Susan Partridge and the Australian Thelma Long, won sets in successive round from Miss Connolly by exploiting a slow, highish ball down the middle. They were the only sets taken from the wonder player in singles at this or any of the two subsequent Wimbledons.

Yet in spite of Miss Connolly's iron skill from the back, her capacity in the forecourt and as a doubles player was slight. In 1953 there was the most extraordinary women's doubles first of all time. Shirley Fry and Doris Hart won for the third successive year, as everyone expected. They came to the final against Miss Connolly and Julie Sampson having lost but four games in all. In the title match they lost no more. They won with a devastating 6-0 6-0 — and that with the world's invincible on the other side of the net!

After her third singles victory in 1954, Miss Connolly broke her leg in a riding accident and never played again. Tragically she died in 1969 of cancer. Her vacant throne was filled by Louise Brough in 1955 who, beating the ambidexterous Beverly Fleitz in a memorably good final, gained her 13th and last Wimbledon title.

After Vic Seixas had replaced Sedgman as men's singles champion in 1953, the event threw up its most popular winner for

years — Drobny, a refugee from Czechoslovakia and classified, because of his passport, as Egyptian. Drobny's epic contest with Patty was the major happening before Seixas stole through to win.

It was in the third round and Drobny began against Patty, his friend and doubles partner, at five o'clock. It was in the darkening shadow that Drobny eventually prised his famous victory, at 9.15p.m. The score was 8-6 16-18 3-6 12-10 after saving three match points in the fourth set and three more in the fifth. It was surging, climactic stuff from first to last and there were 93 games of it, at that time a Wimbledon record.

The Management committee recognised the quality of the duel by presenting both with inscribed gold cigarette cases.

So when Drobny won the title one year later it was felt he was no more than getting a just reward for his heroism. Drobny won as the lowest seed of all time. He was number 11 out of 12. His final was against Ken Rosewall. The score was 13-11 4-6 6-2 9-7. The 58 games made it the longest final on record.

Marion Anthony Trabert, the man from Cincinatti who won in 1955, could be the most underrated champion of all, perhaps because he was all efficiency with a heavy backhand and eschewed spectacular overtones. He did not lose a set in winning and nor did he when he took his own American title later in the year.

Trabert

This decade of American domination ended in a note of British glory. For the first time since 1937 a title was kept at home. It was the women's double, won by Angela Mortimer and Anne Shilcock, and it was an all-British final against Shirley Bloomer and Pat Ward. But that was one title out of 50, of which the U.S. claimed 38!

Dress designer Teddy
Tinling was for years the
arbiter of Wimbledon's
fashion on the court. This
picture of 1946 (with Tinling
sporting his uniform jacket
as Lt. Col. in the Intelligence
Corps) pre-dates the events
of 1949 when his lace
panties creation for
'Gorgeous Gussie' Moran
lost him his post as one of
the referee's assistants.

1946

The all dominant
American women of 1946.
From left to right Pat Todd,
Louise Brough, Pauline Betz,
Dodo Bundy, Margaret
Osborne and Doris Hart.
They lost only to each
other.

1946

Pauline Betz conquered
Wimbledon at her first
attempt in 1946. She was
the spear head of
American domination for
a decade.

1946

Jack Kramer and Tom
Brown, finalists in 1947.
Kramer beat his fellow
American 6–1 6–3 6–2 in
only 48 minutes.

1946

The finalists of 1946. Pauline
Betz (left) beat Louise
Brough 6–2 6–4.

1946

The Australian Geoff Brown
electrified spectators with
his lightning serving in
1946. His defeat in the final
by the Frenchman Yvon
Petra was a complete
reversal of form.

1946

Jack Kramer, the devastating winner of the men's singles in 1947, won against his compatriot Tom Brown in only 48 minutes.

1947

The American Frank
Parker was better on slow
hard courts rather than fast
grass. The Swede Lennart
Bergein beat him 5–7 7–5
9–7 0–6 10–8 in the
fourth round

1948

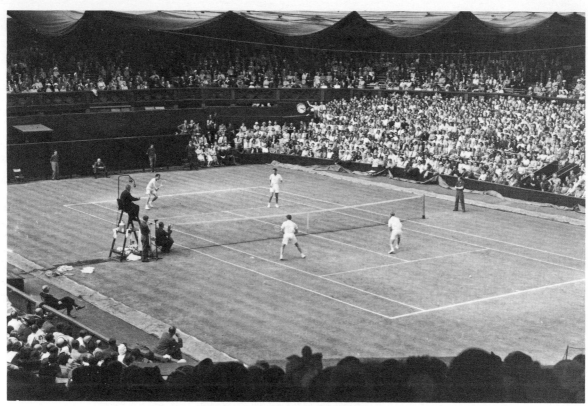

The stirring men's doubles
final of 1948. The Australians
John Bromwich and Frank
Sedgman beat the
Americans Tom Brown
and Gardner Mulloy 5–7
7–5 7–5 9–7.

1948

Bob Falkenburg snatched victory from nowhere in the men's singles final of 1948 when this tall American beat the Australian John Bromwich 7–5 0–6 6–2 3–6 7–5 from 2–5 and three match points at 3–5 in the final set.

1948

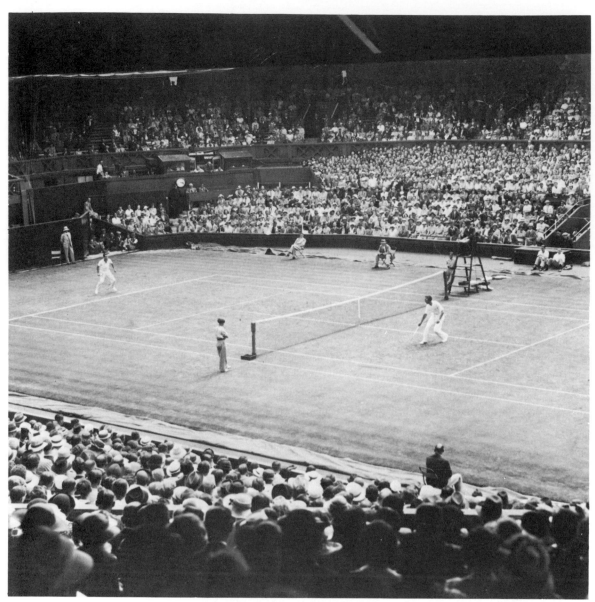

The Centre Court in 1949 —
jam packed as usual. By
the late 1940's the crowds
had begun to be
uncomfortably large.

1949

The American Frank
Parker was a quarter-
finalist in 1949, losing to the
South African Eric Sturgess.
He won the men's doubles
with Pancho Gonzales.

1949

The women's final in 1949 was one of the all time classics. Louise Brough (left) beat Margaret du Pont 10-8 1-6 10-8.

1949

Jaroslav Drobny, then of Czechoslovakia, was competing for the sixth time when he reached the final in 1949. Ted Schroeder was playing for his first and only time and he won 3–6 6–0 6–3 4–6 6–4. Drobny is on the left in both pictures. The Duchess of Kent presented Schroeder with the trophy.

1949

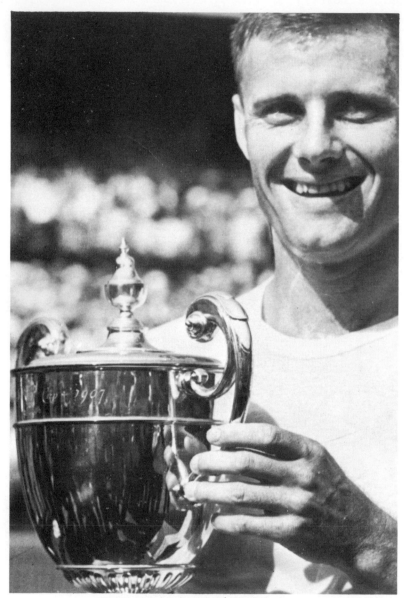

Winner at his first and only
challenge — the
Californian Ted Schroeder

1949

'Gorgeous Gussie' Moran
had her best Wimbledon
in 1950 when she reached
the quarter-final.

1950

71

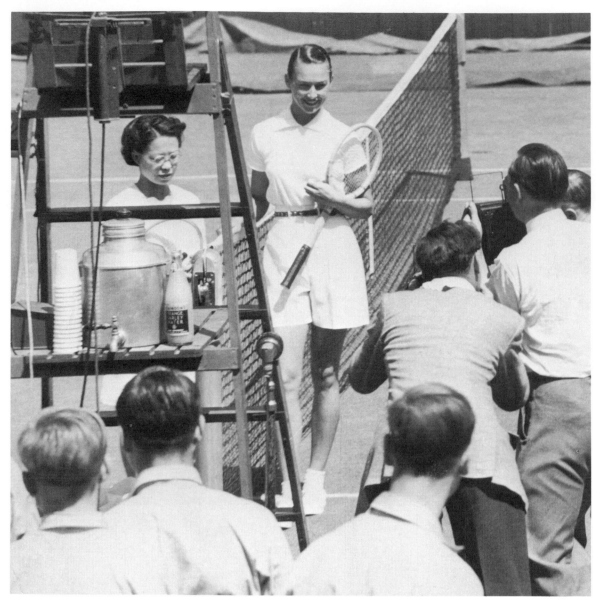

'Gorgeous Gussie' Moran in 1950 was the most photographed player at Wimbledon.

1950

1950

John Bromwich (far left) and Adrian Quist made history by winning the first all Australian men's doubles final against Geoff Brown and Bill Sidwell in 1950. 12 years before in 1938 they took their first Australian title.

Geoff Brown and Bill
Sidwell featured in the all
Australian men's doubles
final of 1950. They lost to
John Bromwich and
Adrian Quist.

1950

1950

Louise Brough (right) beat
Margaret du Pont 6–1 3–6
6–1 to win for the third
year in a row in 1950.

A great player and a great
favourite, Doris Hart. She
won the singles for the first
time in 1951 and went on to
take the women's and
mixed doubles as well.

1951

Dick Savitt, champion in
1951, was the fifth American
in as many years to take
the singles crown. His
backhand was his most
powerful shot.

1951

Dick Savitt receiving the
singles trophy from the
Duchess of Kent. Ken
McGregor was the beaten
finalist in 1951.

1951

The doubles winners 1952,
Frank Sedgman and Ken
McGregor. Sedgman was
the triple champion.

1952

Frank Sedgman, champion
in 1952, was the first
Australian victor since Jack
Crawford in 1933.

1952

1953

Vic Seixas, seen here with
Ken Rosewall (right) won
the men's singles against
Nielsen in 1953.

One of the all time 'greats'.
The incomparable 'Little
Mo' — Maureen Connolly,
unbeaten in singles at
Wimbledon 1952, 1953 and
1954.

1954

Jaroslav Drobny (left) was
playing his third singles
final in 1954 when he beat
the Australian Ken
Rosewall 13–11 4–6 6–2
9–7. Its 58 games was the
longest on record.

1954

83

1954   Jaroslav Drobny was the
most popular singles
winner for years when,
seeded 11th, he won in 1954.

The champions in their
social glory. Maureen
Connolly and Jaroslav
Drobny at the L.T.A. Ball,
Grosvenor House, after their
victories in 1954.

1954

The mixed doubles was won by the Americans Vic Seixas and Doris Hart, for the third year in harness and for the fifth time by Miss Hart.

1955

British glories! The women's doubles final 1955 was all British and Angela Mortimer (far right) partnered Anne Shilcock to beat Shirley Bloomer and Pat War (far left) 7–5 6–1.

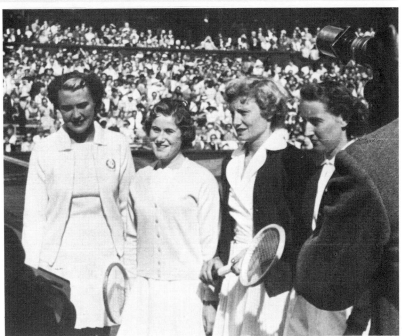

1955

Rex Hartwig partnered his
fellow Australian Lew Hoad
to take the doubles in 1955.

1955

With the retirement of
Maureen Connolly 1955
saw the come back of
Louise Brough. She won for
the fourth year.

1955

Tony Trabert took the men's singles back to America and did not lose a set. In the final he beat an unseeded finalist, the Dane Kurt Nielsen.

1955

THE AUSTRALIANS FIGHT BACK
1956-1967

This was the last dozen years of Wimbledon as the peak of amateur lawn tennis. The world heaved and groaned with the political efforts to remedy the hypocritical nonsenses of sham-amateurism.

The growth of its popularity was unabated. In 1967 the total attendance exceeded 300,000 for the first time. It had gone over 200,000 first in 1932.

No less than nine of the men's singles champions were Australian: the mighty Lew Hoad in 1956 and 1957, Ashley Cooper in 1958, Neale Fraser in 1960, the great, great Rod Laver in 1961 and 1962, the dashing Roy Emerson in 1964 and 1965, the solid John Newcombe in 1967.

memorable also. It was remarkable in its winners, the Americans Gardnar Mulloy and Budge Patty, both seemingly past their best. Mulloy, an outstanding extrovert and talker on the court, was 43 years 7 months old. Among men there has been none more venerable.

Even more remarkable was the interruption. A woman, brandishing a banner decrying the evils of international banking, ran across the Centre Court to the Royal Box, occupied by Queen Elizabeth. Yet even with this unique demonstration, basic standards of good behaviour were followed. She had waited until the players were changing ends!

The left-handed genius of Laver impressed itself on the meeting in 1959 when, unseeded, he reached the singles final and lost to the Peruvian-born Alex

Hoad

Hoad, in winning his 1957 final against Cooper, put up the most thrustful, over-whelming display of powerhouse lawn tennis that had been seen for years and it remains an abiding memory. At the time, he was already committed to signing a professional contract with Jack Kramer.

"You realise," Hoad was told before the match, "that you get $100,000 if you lose, $125,000 if you win." Hoad, with his iron wrist, was one of the all-time greats.

The 1957 men's doubles final was

Olmedo. A year later he lost his second final, this time to another left-hander, the tall Neale Fraser from Melbourne.

Fraser ranked as a lucky champion. In the quarter-final against the American Earl Buchholz, he survived with a winning score of 4-6 6-3 4-6 15 games all (ret'd), having had six match points against him. Cramp made Buchholz helpless in the decisive stages.

Laver's second year as champion, 1962, had British warmth in the men's singles.

Frazer

Uniquely there were two home players in the last eight: Bobby Wilson, who was there for the third time, and the big-serving Mike Sangster. The latter went on to become a semi-finalist and one had to go back to 1938 to find anything as good.

McKinley

Chuck McKinley, who gallivanted about the forecourt like a spring, replaced Laver

when that Australian had donned the mantle of professionalism. There was nothing quite like his 1963 triumph in that he never met one of the eight seeds and that no seeded player met another at any stage. The losing finalist was Australian, Fred Stolle, who went on to equal Von Cramm's unenviable pre-war record of being the losing finalist in three successive years.

The victor for the next two years was the dashing Emerson. The odds against his winning three years running were small but in 1966 he was unlucky in the quarter-final. Against his compatriot Owen Davidson he chased a drop shot too enthusiastically and injured himself against the net post.

Accordingly the way opened up for the victory of the Spanish Manuel Santana, who declaimed, "Grass is for cows, not tennis". But his touch genius made itself triumphant none the less. The following meeting he did what no defending champion had done before — he lost in the first round.

Santana

The women's singles had its 13th consecutive American champion with

Shirley Fry in 1956, its 14th and 15th when Althea Gibson, tall and athletic and black, succeeded her. The sequence was ended by the Brazilian Maria Bueno. It was at her second attempt when this majestic player, whose margin of error was dangerously low, was as successful on the court as her strokes were imperious.

Bueno

Miss Bueno kept her crown in 1960, a year notable for the most outré mixed doubles final. The winners were Laver and the American Darlene Hard and they survived three match points to beat Australian Bob Howe and Miss Bueno 13-11 3-6 8-6. The oddity of it was not the match points saved but the infliction on Miss Hard of uniquely feminine physical distress. She fled to the dressing room, leaving umpire, her opponents and the crowd in puzzled wonderment. The match was resumed after about five minutes without a word!

In 1961 British patriots had their greatest moment for years. A home winner of the women's singles was assured when both Christine Truman and Miss Mortimer came through to the final. None was ever more popular than Miss Truman, the universal "girl next door", who had never done anything unsporting in her life and who had brave, aggressive tactics in which she flogged the ball with a superb forehand that was created by the light of nature.

The world longed for her to be a winner and she won the first set and was within a point of leading 5-3 in the second when, recoiling to retrieve a lob, she fell and jarred herself. She was confronted at the next point with a drop shot and Miss Mortimer deservedly won the title. But she was constrained to say afterwards, "Christine got the sympathy but I got the championship".

Susman

After 1962, when the Californian Karen Susman won without the loss of a set, and was not very popular because of her habit of dilly-dallying to reserve her energies, the great Australian Margaret Smith, later Margaret Court, came into her own. This was athleticism and gym-work and hard training personified. She and Miss Bueno and Billie Jean Moffitt, who became Mrs. King, brought a trinity of rivalry unsurpassed in the history of the game.

The sequence of their Wimbledon success was Miss Bueno in 1964, after which she dropped out of things, Miss Smith in 1965 and then Mrs. King in 1966 and 1967. Mrs. King had won her first title, the women's doubles, with Karen Susman in 1961. It was the initiation of a unique record which extended into the open era.

The dogged Vic Seixas,
having won the mixed
doubles three years
running with Doris Hart,
took it for the fourth time in
1956 with Shirley Fry.

1956

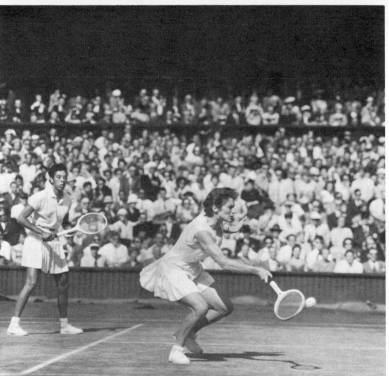

Althea Gibson, the first black American to be champion, partnered the British Angela Buxton to win the women's doubles in 1956. Finalists were Fay Muller and Daphne Seeney of Australia.

1956

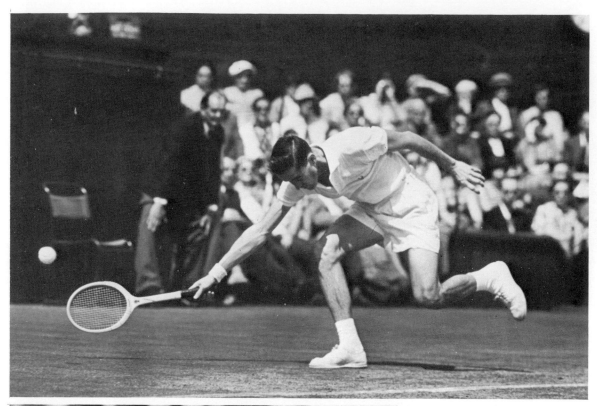

Ken Rosewall (above) and
Lew Hoad (left) were
destined not to appear in
the same Wimbledon
Championships until the
onset of open tennis.
Together they won the
men's doubles.

1956

The pattern of American dominance was maintained with Shirley Fry winning the women's singles in 1956. Angela Buxton was the first Briton to contest the final since 1939.

1956

99

A giant of a champion!
Lew Hoad won the singles
for the first time in 1956.

Lew with Mrs Hoad, the
former Jennifer Staley, who
was herself a first class
player.

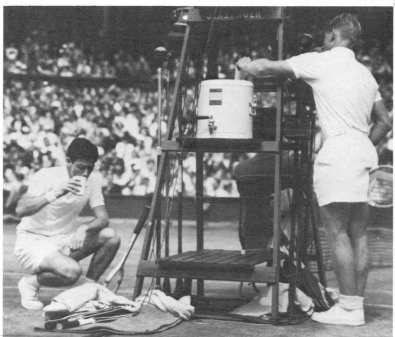

In the final Hoad beat his
doubles partner Ken
Rosewall 6–2 4–6 7–5
6–4.

1956

Darlene Hard, beaten in the singles final but triumphant in the women's doubles, played in her third final, the mixed. She partnered the Australian Mervyn Rose to take her second title.

1957

Darlene Hard (left) was
beaten by Althea Gibson
in the final of the singles
but paired with her to
triumph in the women's
doubles.

1957

Americans Budge Patty (left) and Gardner Mulloy broke new ground by winning the men's doubles in 1957. Not only were they unseeded but Mulloy at the age of 43 years 7 months was the oldest man to win a championship.

1957

The women's singles final
of 1957 reverted to this
familiar all American
pattern. Althea Gibson
beat Darlene Hard (above)
forthrightly by 6–3 6–2.

1957

The second triumph in singles for Lew Hoad. In 1957 he won a devastating contest against his compatriot Ashley Cooper.

1957

Neither Shirley Bloomer nor
Billy Knight, (left) two
popular British players,
were destined to win a
Wimbledon title. In 1958
they played the semi-final
of the mixed and lost to the
Dane Kurt Nielsen and the
black American Althea
Gibson.

1958

Althea Gibson won the
singles for the second time
in 1958. She won the
doubles with the majestic
Brazilian Maria Bueno who
made her first appearance
that year. In the final they
beat Margaret du Pont
and her fellow American
Margaret Varner.

1958

Sweden had its glory in 1958 and, as the year before, it was an unseeded pair who won the men's doubles — Sven Davidson (left) and Ulf Schmidt. Ashley Cooper and Neale Fraser were the surprise losers in a three set final.

1958

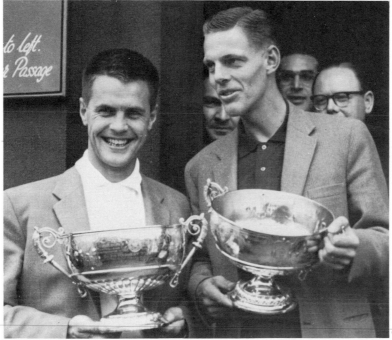

There was rarely a doubt about Althea Gibson's singles victory in 1958 and she lost only one set, to Shirley Bloomer in the quarter-final. But at nearly 31 success had come later than to most.

1958

Ashley Cooper in 1958 was
able to forget his rousting
by Lew Hoad the year
before when he won
another all Australian final
against Neale Fraser.

1958

A famous name was
inscribed on the honours'
board in 1959. The
Australian left hander Rod
Laver won the mixed
doubles with the American
Darlene Hard.

1959

Americans Darlene Hard
and Jean Arth won the
women's doubles in 1959.
British hopes ran high for
an outstanding favourite,
Christine Truman was in
the final with Beverly Fleitz
(U.S.) The all American
partnership won 2−6 6−2
6−3.

1959

(From the left) Bob Mark,
Rod Laver, Neale Fraser
and Roy Emerson who
fought the all Australian
men's doubles final for 1959.
Emerson and Fraser were
the winners by 8–6 6–3
14–16 9–7.

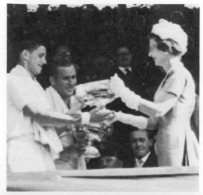

1959

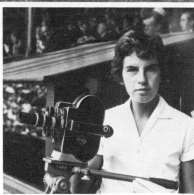

Maria Bueno, the most majestic if not the most consistent of post 1946 players, won Wimbledon at her second attempt in 1959. In Brazil they issued a postage stamp with her portrait to mark the event! 1959

Alex Olmedo was Peruvian born but his tennis was nurtured in California. No one could stop his dynamic volleying.

1959

One of the finest mixed
doubles finals ever played.
Rod Laver (far right) and
Darlene Hard beat Bob
Howe (far left), a fellow
Australian, and Maria
Bueno, 13–11 3–6 9–5.

1960

Darlene Hard and Maria Bueno were never in danger in the women's doubles. In the title match they took the measure of the notable South African partnership Sandra Reynolds and Renee Schuurman 6–4 6–0.

1960

The Mexican Rafael Osuna 1960
(foreground) and the
American Dennis Ralston
took the men's doubles. The
first time challenger Ralston
was 17 years 11 months old,
the youngest male
champion ever.

Maria Bueno in 1960 was as dashing and as invincible as the previous year.

1960

Two Australian left
handers, Neale Fraser (left)
and Rod Laver (above top),
played the singles final of
1960 and Laver lost for the
second year. It was many
years before he was
brought down at
Wimbledon again.

1960

Bob Howe, Edda Buding,
Lesley Turner and Fred
Stolle (from left to right)
were the mixed finalists in
1961 and only the German
Fraulein Buding averted a
clean Australian sweep.
Stolle and Miss Turner took
the title.

1961

1961

Karen Hantze and her fellow Californian Billie Jean Moffitt won the women's doubles. They were unseeded. For Miss Moffitt, aged 17, it was her first challenge and her first (of 20!) championships.

The men's doubles revert to an old story, an all Australian final. Neale Fraser (left) and Roy Emerson won against Fred Stolle and Bob Hewitt (then Australian) by 6-4 6-8 6-4 6-8 8-6 for their second success in three years.

1961

127

The best for Britain since 1914! In the all British women's singles final Angela Mortimer came from behind to beat Christine Truman 4–6 6–4 7–5.

1961

The first of a long run! Rod Laver won, after two losing finals, his first singles championship in 1961. He was not to be beaten until the fourth round against Roger Taylor in 1970.

1961

Neale Fraser, Ann Haydon,
Margaret du Pont and
Dennis Ralston (left to right)
were the finalists in the
mixed. Fraser and Mrs du
Pont won after a notable
final, 2–6 6–3 13–11, and
at 44 years 4 months Mrs
du Pont, the singles
champion of 1947, became
the oldest champion.

1962

Having won at their first attempt the year before Billie Jean Moffitt and Karen Hantze, now Karen Susman, repeated their success in the women's doubles.

1962

Bob Hewitt, then
representing Australia, and
Fred Stolle, won the men's
doubles for the first time.
Boro Jovanovic and Nikki
Pilic of Yugoslavia were
unexpected finalists.

1962

Karen Susman took the singles crown at the age of 19. She was the third Californian champion coached by 'Teach' Tennant who also taught Alice Marble and Maureen Connolly.

1962

Rod Laver took the men's singles almost as a matter of course. It was his first 'Grand Slam' year.

1962

Margaret Smith partnered
her fellow Australian Ken
Fletcher to take the mixed,
the first of many triumphs
as a pair. They did not lose
a set.

1963

The majestic Maria Beuno and Darlene Hard won the women's doubles for the second time. They did not lose a set but the final, against Robin Ebbern and Margaret Smith, was tough — 8–6 9–7.

1963

For the fourth time in five years an unseeded pair became men's doubles champions, the dynamic Rafael Osuna and his fellow Mexican Antonio Palafox.

1963

They were rivals for a decade. Margaret Smith won the first of her three singles crowns by beating Billie Jean Moffitt 6-3 6-4.

1963

Chuck McKinley won the men's singles for the U.S. He was seeded 4th. But he never met another seeded player and nor did any seed play another!

1963

The mixed doubles line up
— Ken Fletcher, Margaret
Smith, Lesley Turner and
Fred Stolle (from left to
right). Stolle and Miss
Turner repeated their
triumph of 1961.

1964

Margaret Smith and Lesley Turner were unbeaten in the women's doubles. The Americans Billie Jean Moffitt and Karen Susman were the losing finalists.

1964

The Australians dominated the men's doubles. Hewitt and Stolle won for the second time in a final against Roy Emerson and Ken Fletcher.

1964

Only Maria Bueno prevented Wimbledon being claimed as Australian territory. This year the Brazilian won the singles for the third time.

1964

Mobile Roy Emerson won the sixth all Australian men's singles final against Fred Stolle 6–4 12–10 4–6 6–3.

1964

Billie Jean Moffit and
Maria Bueno came
together to win the doubles
as an American-Brazilian
team.

1965

Australian command of
the men's doubles was
firmly maintained. John
Newcombe and the left
handed Tony Roche had
the first of their victories.

1965

Margaret Smith took her
singles title number two,
this time without losing a
set. She reversed the
outcome of the previous
year by beating Maria
Bueno.

1965

Roy Emerson had the second of his fleet footed singles victories.

(left)
Fred Stolle

1965

Margaret Smith was denied the singles crown but she won the mixed with Ken Fletcher for the second year running and the third time in all.

1966

Nancy Richey partnered
Maria Bueno to win the
women's doubles and the
final against Margaret
Smith and Judy Tegart was
tough.

1966

John Newcombe won the men's doubles for the second year with a different partner, Ken Fletcher.

1966

Billie Jean Moffitt, now Mrs King, won the singles for the first time. Maria Bueno, playing her third successive final, was runner-up for the second year.

1966

157

A touch genius, Manuel
Santana of Spain, won the
men's singles. The final, in
which he beat the
American Dennis Ralston,
was one of the friendliest
ever played.

1966

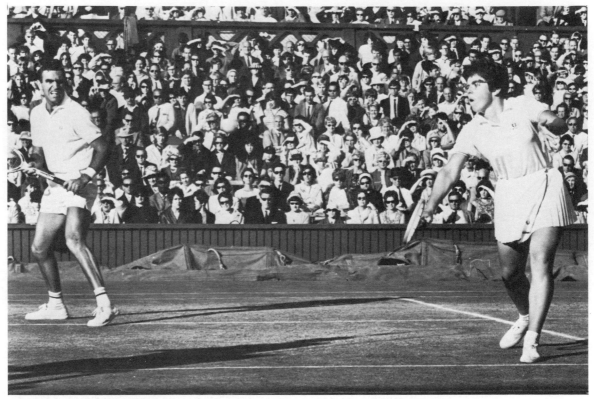

Billie Jean King was with
the Australian Owen
Davidson in the mixed
and she made herself a
triple champion, the first
since Frank Sedgman in
1952.

1967

A notable women's
doubles pairing, Rosemary
Casals and Billie Jean King,
proved itself for the first
time. In the final they beat
the title holders, Maria
Bueno and Nancy Richey,
9–11 6–4 6–2.

1967

Bob Hewitt was now under South African colours and he and Frew McMillan took the doubles for the first time without losing a set.

1967

There was no stopping
Billie Jean King. She did not
lose a set in the singles,
where the British Ann
Jones was the finalist.

1967

163

John Newcombe won the last men's singles of an 'amateur' Wimbledon. His final win against the German Wilhelm Bungert was one of the most one sided of all time.

1967

OPEN TO ALL
1968-1980

There had been pressure to make lawn tennis open for many years, not least from the Wimbledon chairman Herman David, before the change was effected by unilateral and illegal action by the British L.T.A. in 1967. It forced the hand of the International Federation and the world's ruling body capitulated to a fait accompli at a special meeting in Paris on 30th March 1968.

Wimbledon's first open in 1968 opened a treasure box of riches. Most notable among the professionals allowed back into the fold, for their skills were still razor-sharp, were Rod Laver, Ken Rosewall and Richard Gonzales. Laver had not been there since 1962 and Rosewall not since 1956. Gonzales had been absent since 1949.

There had not been such a vibrant tournament for years. As it happened, Rosewall did not justify his second seeding. Nor did Gonzales fill his role as number eight. Laver, seeded one, picked up where he had left off in 1962 and his two successive wins were made into three. He was under much pressure but, curiously, his easiest victory was in the final against his fellow Australian left-hander Tony Roche.

Laver's stature as a giant was made evident one year later. He was given a scare in the second round by the Indian

Laver

Premjit Lall, who won the first two sets. He went on to win a marvellous semi-final against Arthur Ashe (who had become the first U.S. Open champion in 1968) in which the pace hitting of the first two sets, shared 2-6 6-2 before Laver went on to win 9-7 6-0, was unparalleled in its intensity. Laver beat Newcombe in the final.

This effort of Laver was part of his Grand Slam sequence for the year. No-one had achieved it twice.

There was a backdrop to Laver's great effort in 1969 with a match which, in its intensity of excitement and duration, was without equal. At the age of 41 Gonzales, one of the world's greatest players of all time — and denied the best exhibition of his skill by the division in the game — paraded his richest qualities on the stage best fitted the show them, the Centre Court.

Against Charles Pasarell, 16 years his junior, he lost a surging first set 22-24 and an ill-tempered second in fading light by 1-6 He came back the next day to win 16-14 6-3 11-9, saving seven match points on the way; twice coming back from love-40 on his serve in the final set. These 112 games were a peak of Wimbledon's drama and, during the five hours the match lasted, the standard — often superb — never fell short of good. No greater number of games was ever played in a match at Wimbledon.

Laver lost his invincibility in 1970 and was beaten for the first time in the singles since the final of 1960 when Yorkshire's Roger Taylor won 4-6 6-4 6-1 on the middle Saturday. None the less the Australia saga was not over. Taylor yielded to the classic craft of Rosewall in the semi-final and in turn Rosewall went down to the insistent Newcombe in the final. Rosewall had last been at that stage in 1956.

Rosewall

Newcombe was champion again in 1971. There had been 13 singles titles for Australia since 1956. He might in 1972 have won for the third year running and the fourth time in all.

But in 1972 politics reared an ugly head. Because of the unease between the I.L.T.F. and the rising World Championship concern, those players under professional contract were barred. Newcombe could not enter.

because of rain.

The ugly politics of 1972 were resolved. Those of 1973 were catastrophic.

The Association of Tennis Professionals, formed in September 1972, objected to the suspension of the Yugoslav Nikki Pilic. This was primarily a domestic concern of the Yugoslav ruling body but their discipline was upheld by the I.L.T.F. and Wimbledon in turn followed regulations.

The dispute culminated in a boycott

Nastase

Stan Smith of America won the title, his success notable on two counts. One was the superb quality of the final against Ilie Nastase, the brilliant Rumanian then more or less at his peak of genius, which Smith won 7-5 in the fifth set. The second was the fact of its being played on Sunday, with free admission for a delighted crowd,

being called by the players' "union" on the day when the draw should have been made. At a stroke Wimbledon lost 79 of the leading players. Just three men, all of whom were subsequently fined, did not obey the A.T.P. call — the British Roger Taylor, Ilie Nastase and the Australian Ray Keldie.

Compared with what it should have been, the standard of the men's field was diminished to negligible standards. Nastase, promoted to top seed, did not justify that status. Taylor, a British hero who was greeted with cheers every time he showed himself, got to the semi-final. The Czech Jan Kodes was the main benefactor of the ban and took the title against a Russian finalist, Alex Metreveli.

Wimbledon's chairman, Herman David, behaved magnanimously. He said, "There will be no recriminations," and nor were there any.

The loyalty of Wimbledon's spectators was a revelation. Attendance was 300,172, the second highest figure to that time.

The boycott traumas of 1973 had not affected the women in any way. Nor, for that matter, had the transition from a technically amateur to an open status in 1968. The first of the women's open champions was the ubiquitous Billie Jean King who, having been a triple champion in 1967, took the singles for the third successive year in 1968.

British enthusiasts were cock-a-hoop in 1969. Ann Jones, whose left-handed guile had taken her to the semi-final for the seventh time in 1968, was inspired to her most aggressive and effective form when it mattered most. She beat Margaret Court in the semi-final and then Mrs. King in the final to become the second post-war British winner.

Her successors were Australian, Margaret Court having her third victory in 1970. She beat Mrs. King 14-12 11-9 and its 46 games were the greatest number ever played in the final. It was probably the greatest in aggressive standards too. Such sustained virility had never been seen between two women before.

There was charm and natural genius to replace one Australian women's champion with another in 1971. At 19, the captivating Evonne Goolagong, who

Cawley

King

actually seemed to enjoy playing, whether in victory or defeat, and had everybody falling in love with her, was the winner.

Then, in 1972 when Chris Evert made her debut as a novice American and reached the semi-final, Mrs. King reeled off singles title number four. One year later she made it number five, beating Miss Evert in the final. The losing semi-finalists were Mrs. Court, who lost to Miss Evert, and Miss Goolagong. With so rich a women's field in 1973, the paucity of the men's hardly mattered.

Stylistically 1974 was a landmark year. Jimmy Connors won the men's singles. Miss Evert the women's. Nothing could have been more romantic, since at that time

Connors

they were engaged to be married. But nothing could have been more unorthodox. Each was double-fisted on the backhand. It became the norm in the game from that time on.

Rosewall was in the final against Connors and it was one-sided. None the less, all records were broken. It was Rosewall's fourth final. The first had been in 1954, twenty years before. Who else but so superb a stylist would be as good at 39 as he was at 19?

Ashe

Arthur Ashe, the first black American man to do so well, brilliantly dispossessed Connors in the 1975 final, tactically running rings around his more powerful opponent. Mrs. King took the women's singles almost as a matter of routine. It was for the sixth time and, with 19 Wimbledon titles in all, she drew level with the record set in 1934 by her fellow Californian Elizabeth Ryan.

Miss Evert was the 1976 singles champion. In 1977 the British women's game shone again, appropriately in what was Wimbledon's centenary celebration year and the Silver Jubilee of Queen Elizabeth.

Wade

Her Majesty was present in the Royal Box to see the gallant Virginia Wade in her finest moment, winning the singles at her 19th attempt. She won the final against the Dutch Betty Stove and it was a long way short of a great match. But the enthusiasm that greeted Miss Wade's triumph provided one of Wimbledon's noisiest and most patriotic moments.

Navratilova

No rival could contain the volleying insurgence of Martina Navratilova in 1978 and 1979. What she had learned under Czech training had been polished under American free enterprise.

Elizabeth Ryan was at Wimbledon in 1979, mentally sharp but physically immobile at the age of 87. She had remarked more than once, "I hope I never live to see my record broken". On July 6th she collapsed in the dressing room and was dead on reaching hospital. On July 7th Billie Jean King won the women's doubles with Miss Navratilova and furthered her tally of Wimbledon titles to a record 20.

It seemed in 1980 that Miss Navratilova had, like a fast bowler, burned herself out. Evonne Goolagong, now Evonne Cawley and the mother of a young daughter, came back in happy triumph. She was the first mother to win since Dorothea Lambert Chambers in 1914.

The records achieved at Wimbledon in recent years, however, belong most richly to the Swede Bjorn Borg. His first singles win was 1976 when he did not lose a set. He yielded six sets in 1977, three in 1978, six in 1979 and four in 1980. But no-one beat him.

Five Wimbledon championships in sequence after playing through is a record of staggering proportions. The consistency of his top spin expertise, both forehand and double-fisted backhand, has been breathtaking.

In 1977 John McEnroe set the world upside down. This forthright young American, who suffered fools by no means gladly, was sent to Wimbledon as a junior and survived the qualifying competition to take part in the championships proper. Then, though a mere junior and a mere qualifier, he reached the semi-final, losing only to Connors!

Borg, whose finals were first against Nastase in 1976, then twice against Connors and fourth against Roscoe Tanner, clashed with McEnroe in the title match for 1980.

Of the many great contests played at Wimbledon, this probably was the greatest. Borg was a great fighting machine and probably rather tougher than McEnroe. The fourth set tie break (the system was introduced at Wimbledon in 1971) was not resolved until 18-16. Borg won 1-6 7-5 6-3 6-7 8-6. It gave Borg, no more than 24 years old, his fifth singles title.

The first open Wimbledon brought no change in the mixed doubles. Ken Fletcher and Margaret Smith, now Mrs Court, won for the fourth time in six years.

1968

Billie Jean King and
Rosemary Casals
continued their domination
of the women's doubles.

1968

Australians John
Newcombe and Tony
Roche came back into
harness to win the men's
doubles for the second
time.

1968

For the women the first
open Wimbledon was the
same as before. Billie Jean
King won the singles for
the third year.

1968

Rod Laver, the first singles champion at the first open Wimbledon. He resumed where he left off in 1962, when he had become a professional.

1968

Jack Kramer (left) and Dan
Maskell had a listening
public of millions for their
B.B.C. T/V commentaries.

1968

Ann Jones not only had
the finest success of her
career by winning the
singles at the age of 30 but
she also won the mixed
doubles with Australian
Fred Stolle.

1969

Margaret Court and Judy
Tegart won the women's
doubles by winning the
final against the
Americans Peggy Michel
and Patti Hogan.

1969

John Newcombe and
Tony Roche took the men's
doubles for the third time
and conceded only one set
in all. The final was against
the Dutch Tom Okker and
the American Marty
Riessen.

1969

Ann Jones played the most aggressive and most effective tennis of her career to win the singles for Britain.

1969

Rod Laver had his last
invincible year, taking the
singles for the fourth time in
four attempts.

1969

The Rumanian Ilie Nastase
had his first success. He
won the mixed doubles
with Rosemary Casals as
an unseeded pair.

1970

Billie Jean King and
Rosemary Casals had their
third joint success in the
women's doubles. This year
they did not lose a set.

1970

It was fourth for Tony
Roche and fifth for John
Newcombe as the
Australians had their fourth
joint success in the men's
doubles.

1970

Margaret Court won the women's singles to be champion for the third time. In the final her victory over Billie Jean King by 14–12 11–9 was among the greatest women's matches of all time.

1970

John Newcombe took the
singles for the second time.
Prince Charles saw him
beat Ken Rosewall in the
final.

1970

Owen Davidson and Billie
Jean King (left) won the
mixed doubles final
against another notable
pairing, Margaret Court
and Marty Riessen. The
score was 3–6 6–2 15–13.

1971

Billie Jean King and
Rosemary Casals won the
women's doubles for the
fourth time in five years.
For Mrs King it was her
seventh triumph in the
event.

1971

Rod Laver had ceased to win the singles. He became men's doubles champion for the first time, with Roy Emerson.

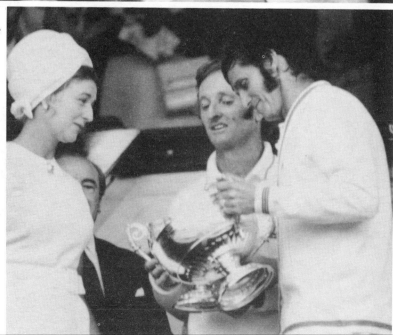

Evonne Goolagong
charmed and delighted
spectators by winning the
singles at only her second
attempt. The Australian,
part aborigine in race, beat
her compatriot Margaret
Court 6–4 6–1 in the final.

1971

197

John Newcombe had his
second singles win in two
years, his third in all.

1971

Rosemary Casals and Ilie
Nastase had their second
success in three years in
the mixed doubles. They
were seeded number two
and did not lose a set.

1972

The Dutch Betty Stove gained her Wimbledon championship crown in the women's doubles with Billie Jean King. For the American it was her 8th win in the event.

1972

A men's doubles final with
a suprisingly one sided
outcome. The Americans
Erik Van Dillen and Stan
Smith (left) failed to win a
set against the South
African Davis Cup pair
Frew McMillan and Bob
Hewitt.

1972

Invincible in singles for the fourth time — Billie Jean King. She beat the defending champion Evonne Goolagong in the final.

1972

Ilie Nastase, arguably one of the greatest touch players of all time, and perhaps the most temperamental, provoked the American Stan Smith into an outstanding men's singles final. He was beaten only 7–5 in the fifth set.

1972

Stan Smith, playing on the Sunday because of rain delays, became men's singles champion at the expense of the Rumanian Ilie Nastase after a five set final that was acknowledged as one of the finest ever played.

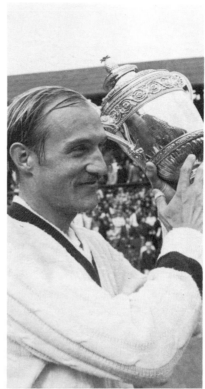

1972

For the second time Billie
Jean King was triple
champion. She had her
third success in the mixed
with Owen Davidson and
acquired her 17th
Wimbledon title.

1973

Rosemary Casals and Billie
Jean King resumed their
partnership in the women's
doubles and won for the
fifth time. For Mrs King it
was her eighth win in the
event.

1973

In the boycott year the men's strength was sparse. But the Rumanian Ilie Nastase and the American Jimmy Connors, who won the doubles, would always have been a formidable pair in any field.

1973

There was no diminution of the women's field. Billie Jean King was unbeaten in the singles for the fifth time.

1973

The Czech Jan Kodes was lucky to be able to benefit from the diminished strength of the men's field but he was a good champion none the less and won the final against a Soviet challenger, Alex Metreveli.

1973

210

Owen Davidson and Billie
Jean King won the mixed
for the fourth time.

1974

Australia paired with the U.S. to win the women's doubles — Evonne Goolagong and Peggy Michel.

1974

John Newcombe and
Tony Roche added more to
the records. The
invulnerable Australians
won the men's doubles for
the 5th time.

1974

Chris Evert won the women's singles at 19, winning against a Soviet finalist, Olga Morozova. She had already won the Italian and French titles but had not yet won her native American crown.

1974

The singles triumph of
Jimmy Connors was at the
expense of the Australian
Ken Rosewall in a one
sided final. But Rosewall
had broken records by
getting as far. He was 39
years old and competing
in his fourth final since he
was first there in 1954, 20
years before.

1974

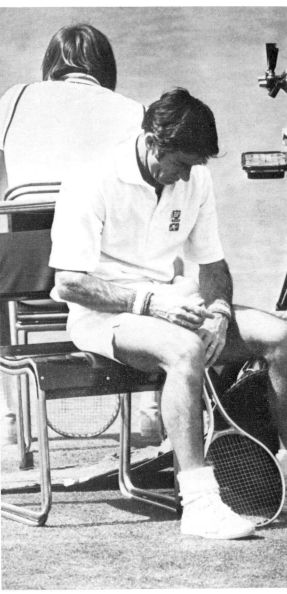

Jimmy Connors won the
men's singles for America,
the triumph for a fighting,
surging player.

1974

Marty Riessen and
Margaret Court were
mixed doubles champions,
Mrs Court taking that title
for the fifth time. It was her
10th and last Wimbledon
championship.

1975

The women's doubles broke new ground. Ann Kiyomura, an American of Japanese origin, and Kazuko Sawamatsu of Japan, beat the French Francoise Durr and the Dutch Betty Stove in the final.

1975

Two New Yorkers, Sandy Mayer and Vitas Gerulaitis, were the first all American partnership since 1957 to take the men's doubles.

1975

Billie Jean King beat Evonne Cawley (the former Miss Goolagong) easily to win the singles for the sixth time and equal Elizabeth Ryan's 1934 record of 19 titles.

1975

Arthur Ashe, the black
American, played a final
of exquisite craft to win the
final against the defending
champion Jimmy Connors.

1975

Arthur Ashe won his singles title at the age of almost 32. It was 1968 when he had his first great success by taking the inaugural U.S. Open.

1975

The Australian Tony Roche
and the French Francoise
Durr were unexpected
mixed doubles champions.
They survived a match
point in the final against
Dick Stockton and
Rosemary Casals.

1976

A refugee from
Czechoslovakia Martina
Navratilova won her first
title when she paired with
Chris Evert to take the
women's doubles. They
had a narrow final win
over Billie Jean King and
Betty Stove.

1976

The American Brian
Gottfried and the Mexican
Raul Ramirez built a solid
partnership that was
rewarded with the men's
doubles.

1976

Chris Evert had her second
singles success. Her final
against Evonne Cawley
was close — 6–3 4–6 8–6.

1976

The first singles win of Bjorn Borg was at the expense of the Rumanian Ilie Nastase, his second loss in the last match. Borg did not lose a set in any round.

1976

Australians Ross Case and
Geoff Masters took the
men's doubles after losing
a close final a year before.
It was the first all Aussie
final since 1970 as they
beat John Alexander and
Phil Dent.

1977

230

John McEnroe (top left and below) broke new ground by qualifying for the Championships and then, though but a junior of 18, reaching the semi-final.

Vitas Gerulaitis lost in the semi-final to Bjorn Borg after playing five of the most sparkling sets seen for years.

1977

Virginia Wade, the brilliant
British women's singles
champion of the
centenary year.

1977

Virginia Wade never
played better in taking the
women's singles for Great
Britain while Queen
Elizabeth II watched her
from the Royal Box in Silver
Jubilee Year. It was eight
years since Ann Jones had
last won for Britain in 1969
at the age of 30 and Miss
Wade did so at 31.

1977

Jimmy Connors (left)
resisted Bjorn Borg as far as
the fifth set. But the Swede
won the final to take the
singles for the second time.

1977

Bjorn Borg was just 21 when
he became the singles
champion for the second
time. This time he lost a
total of six sets.

1977

Billie Jean King got within
one match of taking her
20th championship with
the Australian Ray Ruffels.
But they were beaten in
the final by Frew McMillan
and Betty Stove, mixed
champions for the first time.

1978

236

Australian dominance
moved into new channels
in the women's doubles
where the title was taken
by Kerry Reid (left) and
Wendy Turnbull.

1978

The old guard thrust back
the new generation's
challenge in the final of
the men's doubles. Bob
Hewitt and Frew McMillan
(bottom left and right)
overwhelmed John
McEnroe and Peter
Fleming (top left and right)
by 6–1 6–4 6–2 to win for
the third time.

1978

Chris Evert (above) came
close to being singles
champion for the third
time. Instead Martina
Navratilova was
champion for the first time
when she won the final
2–6 6–4 7–5.

1978

Bjorn Borg making it for the third successive year as singles champion. With this he matched Fred Perry's record of 1936.

1978

Bob Hewitt, now 39 and a
doubles specialist, won the
mixed for the second time
in three years with South
African Greer Stevens.

1979

Title number 20!
Billie Jean King, partnered
by Martina Navratilova,
won the women's doubles
to reach new horizons. The
day before Mrs King did so
the old joint record holder,
Elizabeth Ryan, died in the
dressing room at the age of
87.

1979

Peter Fleming and John
McEnroe make the grade
in the men's doubles. Brian
Gottfried and Raul Ramirez,
the 1976 champions, were
their victims in the final.

1979

With dynamic left handed
aggression Martina
Navratilova became
singles champion for the
second year. Chris Evert
was now Mrs John Lloyd
and could not match her
in the final.

1979

Bjorn Borg makes it singles
championship number
four. He was now level with
Rod Laver in the record
books — four in four
attempts.

1979

Brother and sister won the mixed doubles for the first time. The 17 year old Californian Tracy Austin partnered her elder brother, John, to win after surviving match points in the final against Australians Mark Edmondson and Dianne Fromholtz.

1980

The Americans Kathy
Jordan and Anne Smith
had a tremendous year in
women's doubles and their
climax was at Wimbledon.

1980

Peter McNamara and Paul McNamee, both from Melbourne, were popular winners of the men's doubles.
McNamee, uniquely as a mature player, abandoned an orthodox backhand in favour of playing with two hands.

1980

Evonne Cawley was a tremendously popular winner of the women's singles when she took the crown nine years after being champion in 1971.

1980

Bjorn Borg, breaking all records, won his fifth successive singles after a final against John McEnroe that was arguably the finest of all time. Borg's winning score was 1–6 7–5 6–3 6–7 8–6 with the fourth set tie break extending to 18–16.

1980

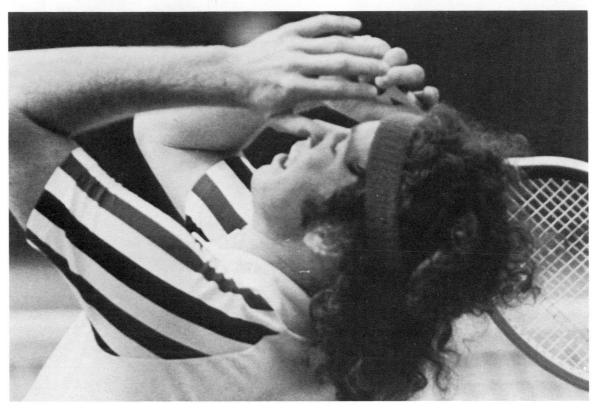

John McEnroe in defeat as
he failed to stop Bjorn Borg.
He began the final less well
regarded than any man
for years and there was
booing. As a gallant loser
he was cheered to the
skies.

1980

Index to Photographs